MAD LIBS
WORKBOOK

GRADE 3 READING

written by Wiley Blevins

MAD LIBS
An Imprint of Penguin Random House LLC, New York

Mad Libs format and text copyright © 2021 by Penguin Random House LLC. All rights reserved.

Mad Libs concept created by Roger Price & Leonard Stern

Cover illustration by Scott Brooks
Interior illustrations by Scott Brooks, Gareth Conway, and Tim Haggerty

Designed by Dinardo Design

Published by Mad Libs,
an imprint of Penguin Random House LLC, New York.
Manufactured in China.

Visit us online at www.penguinrandomhouse.com.

ISBN 9780593222836
3 5 7 9 10 8 6 4 2

MAD LIBS is a registered trademark of Penguin Random House LLC.

WORKBOOK

── INSTRUCTIONS ──

MAD LIBS WORKBOOK is a game for kids who don't like games! It is also a review of the key reading skills for Grade 3. It has both skill practice pages and fun story pages.

RIDICULOUSLY SIMPLE DIRECTIONS:

At the top of each story page, you will find four columns of words, each headed by a symbol. Each symbol represents a type of word, such as a noun (naming word) or a verb (action word). The symbols are:

NOUN	VERB	ADJECTIVE	ADVERB
★	➡	☺	?

MAD LIBS WORKBOOK is fun to play by yourself, but you can also play it with friends! To begin, look at the story on the page below. When you come to a blank space in the story, look at the symbol that appears underneath. Then find the same symbol on this page and pick a word that appears below the symbol. Put that word in the blank space, and cross out the word, so you don't use it again. Continue doing this throughout the story until you've filled in all the spaces. Finally, read your story aloud and laugh!

EXAMPLE:

NOUN ★	VERB ➡	ADJECTIVE ☺	ADVERB ?
~~alien~~	dancing	~~purple~~	happily
~~elephant~~	~~twirling~~	~~spotted~~	carefully
orangutan	tiptoeing	angry	~~frantically~~

We spotted an ___alien___ under the desk. It was ___spotted___ and
      ★   ☺

___twirling___ around. I ___frantically___ left the room and fainted in the
   ➡   ?

hallway. I woke up being stared at by a ___purple___ ___elephant___ .
                                          ☺   ★

QUICK REVIEW

In case you haven't learned about phonics yet, here is a quick review:

There are five **VOWELS**: *a, e, i, o,* and *u.* Each vowel has a short sound and a long sound. The long sound of a vowel says its name. Sometimes the consonants *w* and *y* act as vowels when they are in vowel teams, such as *ow* (snow) and *ay* (play).

All the other letters are called **CONSONANTS.**

A **DIGRAPH** is two or more letters that together make a new sound, such as *sh* (shop) and *ch* (chin).

A **SYLLABLE** is a word part. It has one vowel sound, such as *rain* or *rain/bow.*

A **PREFIX** is a word part added to the beginning of a word, such as *un* in *unhappy.* It changes the word's meaning.

A **SUFFIX** is a word part added to the end of a word, such as *s* (bugs), *ing* (jumping), *ed* (stomped), and *ful* (playful).

In case you have forgotten about the parts of speech, here is a quick review:

A **NOUN** is the name of a person, place, or thing. *Lion, classroom,* and *stove* are nouns.

A **VERB** is an action word. *Skate, jump,* and *scream* are verbs.

An **ADJECTIVE** describes a person, place, or thing. *Soft, fluffy,* and *square* are adjectives.

An **ADVERB** is a word that tells more about a verb or adjective. It can tell how, when, where, or how much. *Slowly, carefully, eagerly,* and *really* are adverbs.

A **PRONOUN** takes the place of a noun in a sentence, such as *I, you, he, she, it, we,* and *they.*

PHONICS AND WORD STUDY

Long Vowels

Each **long vowel** sound says the vowel's name.
Each sound can be spelled many ways.

long a	tr**ai**n, pl**ay**, sl**eigh**, gr**ea**t, t**a**ble, sp**a**ce
long e	str**ee**t, l**ea**f, fi**e**ld, w**e**, k**ey**, happ**y**
long i	br**igh**t, t**ie**, cr**y**, k**i**te, ch**i**ld
long o	g**oa**t, sn**ow**, r**o**pe, g**o**, t**oe**s
long u	f**ew**, m**u**sic, m**u**le, arg**ue**

Add a **long vowel** spelling to finish each picture name.

birthd __ __   p __ __ ntbrush

sixt __ __ n   **16**   p __ __ nut

kn __ __ __ t      cr __ ing

pill __ __   sailb __ __ t

m __ seum      c __ b __

NOUN	VERB	ADJECTIVE	ADVERB
★	→	☺	?
rainbows	dive	tasty	absolutely
starlight	bathe	slimy	rarely
fireflies	float	pickled	sometimes
balloons	sleep	leafy	never

Summertime

Summer is all about the beach! During the daytime, you can _____

→

in the lake or sea and collect seashells and _____ . Then feast on

★

a meal of _____ hot dogs and _____ ice cream.

☺   ☺

They're _____ yummy. After that, rest on a boat as you catch

?

some of the sun's bright rays. As the sunlight slowly slips away, you can rest and view

the nighttime sky. You might see _____ and _____ .

★   ★

All that's left to do is whisper, "Good night." A day at the

beach is _____ a treat—

?

unless it rains, of course!

r-Controlled Vowels

When the letter **r** follows a vowel, it changes the vowel's sound. The spellings **er**, **ir**, and **ur** stand for the same sounds.

f<u>er</u>n   sh<u>ir</u>t   b<u>ur</u>ning

These words have **r-controlled** vowel sounds and spellings, too.

c<u>or</u>n   m<u>ore</u>   r<u>oar</u>   st<u>ar</u>   h<u>air</u>   sh<u>are</u>   p<u>ear</u>

Add an **r-controlled** vowel spelling to finish each picture name.

c __ __ cus    polar b __ __ __

p __ __ ple   guit __ __

unic __ __ n    ch __ __ __ s

sh __ __ k    f __ __ st

NOUN	VERB	ADJECTIVE	ADVERB
★	➡	😊	?
horse	laugh	strange	loudly
governor	nibble	screeching	angrily
slob	dribble	silver	sadly
goose	bark	buttery	quickly

Snow White and the Seven Dwarfs

Snow White wandered deep into the _____ forest. She came upon
😊

a little house. Knock! Knock! The door _____ opened. Before
?

her stood seven _____ men. "Who are you?" Snow White asked.
😊

"I am the _____ doctor," said the first dwarf _____ .
😊   ?

"I am a sleepy _____," said the second dwarf. Then he returned to
★

snoring. The third dwarf stepped forward. "I am a grumpy _____,"
★

he said. "And I don't like to _____ ." "Well...," Snow White started
➡

to say. But the other dwarfs interrupted her. "Enough about you," they said. "We need

to _____ and _____ away. Goodbye!"
➡   ➡

PHONICS AND WORD STUDY

Diphthongs

Some vowel sounds feel like they move around in your mouth.
These spellings stand for those sounds.

b<u>oy</u>　　　　　sp<u>oi</u>led　　　　　s<u>ou</u>th　　　　　fr<u>ow</u>ning

Add one of the above spellings to finish each picture name.

c __ __ b __ __ 　　　　dogh __ __ se

cl __ __ n 　　　　b __ __ ling

m __ __ th 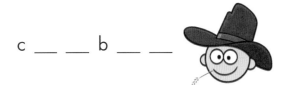　　　　c __ __ ns

j __ __ ful 　　　　cl __ __ dy

fl __ __ ers 　　　　destr __ __ ed

NOUN ★	VERB ➡	ADJECTIVE ☺	ADVERB ?
underwear	frown	fuzzy	angrily
blouses	poo	round	daintily
pickles	meow	soiled	loudly
corduroy	workout	brown	sourly

The Rodeo

Down south in my hometown, we hold a rodeo each

year. And boy is it fun! We have cowboys wearing

_____ _____
         ☺   ★

and _____ hats. When they get into the arena,
                ☺

they will encounter clowns wearing _____ , flags,
                                              ★

barrels, horses, and _____ bulls. The bulls are male
                              ☺

cows with super-sharp horns. They like to charge _____ at
                                                              ?

the clowns. When they do, I shout for the poor clowns to _____
                                                                      ?

_____ before they run. I won't spoil the fun, but sometimes there are
            ➡

surprises. You'll just have to come to the rodeo now to see!

Variant Vowels

The vowel sound in **moon** can be spelled many ways.

sp**oo**n　　　　gl**ue**　　　　gr**ou**p　　　　ch**ew**　　　　J**u**n**e**

The vowel sound in **good** can be spelled many ways.

st**oo**d　　　　　　sh**ou**ld　　　　　　p**u**sh

The vowel sound in **all** can be spelled many ways.

str**aw**　　l**au**nching　　s**al**t　　sm**al**lest　　t**al**king　　b**ough**t　　t**augh**t

Add one of the above spellings to finish each picture name.

br __ __ ms

b __ __ kcase

sidew __ __ k

jigs __ __

kangar __ __

bl __ __

baseb __ __ l

s __ __ sage

s __ __ p

f __ __ tball

NOUN	VERB	ADJECTIVE	ADVERB
★	→	☺	?
spoon	sneeze	crisp	carefully
mushroom	grow	spooky	cheerfully
football	talk	awesome	secretly
sausage	whoosh	salty	naughtily

The Moon

It is a/an _____ fall night, and you _____ look up
☺   ?

in the sky through the new telescope you bought. What can you see? On a night with

no clouds, you should be able to see the moon surrounded by stars. The round moon is

like a _____ in the sky on some nights. On other nights, it looks like
★

a/an _____ _____ . And then there are those rare
☺   ★

nights when it looks like a/an _____ _____
☺   ★

that can _____ . You can see the stars clustered in
→

constellations. Look for the Big Dipper. It looks like a giant

_____ . But keep
★

looking. What else do you see?

PHONICS AND WORD STUDY

Closed Syllables

A **closed syllable** ends in a consonant and has a short vowel sound. Knowing this can help you chunk and read longer words.

<u>lit</u>/tle   <u>nap</u>/<u>kin</u>

Add the missing **closed syllable**.

__ __ __ ten      fos __ __ __

__ __ __ bit      chick __ __

__ __ __ __ __ __ et      in __ __ __ __

__ __ __ __ kin      pen __ __ __

__ __ __ tract      den __ __ __ __

NOUN ★	VERB ➡	ADJECTIVE 😀	ADVERB ?
insects	sing	plastic	Oddly
pumpkins	dance	velvet	Surprisingly
tractors	sew	stuffed	Lately
kittens	talk	empty	Unfortunately

An Odd Farm

Farmer Patrick lives on the oddest farm in the countryside. He has chickens,

pigs, horses, cows, and rabbits in his barns and fields, of course. But he also has

_____ _____ and _____
😀 ★ ★

that can _____ and lay eggs. _____ no one
➡ ?

wants to publish a story or book about his farm. Why? "People will think my head

is _____ ," said a local reporter. The town's
😀

police think it will bring crowds of tourists who will

push to take pictures and _____ with
➡

the farm animals and objects. What do you think?

Would you want to visit this farm?

PHONICS AND WORD STUDY

Open Syllables

An **open syllable** ends in a vowel and has a long vowel sound. Knowing this can help you chunk and read longer words.

<u>se</u>/cret   <u>fi</u>/nal

Add the missing **open syllable**.

__ __ bra    __ __ sic

__ __ by    __ __ ger

__ corn   __ __ ny

__ __ ble    __ __ -yo

__ __ bot    __ __ __ der

NOUN ★	VERB →	ADJECTIVE 😊	ADVERB ?
potatoes	raced	secret	instantly
bagels	tumbled	unusual	immediately
cobras	danced	lethal	suddenly
locusts	wiggled	gigantic	painfully

King Midas and the Golden Touch

Long ago, lived a king named Midas. He had a/an _____ wish:
😊

to turn everything he touched to gold. It would make him the richest ruler in all

the world. One day, his wish came true. He touched his plate filled with

_____ and _____ . Instant gold! He touched his
★   ★

table. Gold. Even his lazy pet lion and baby pony. All _____ gold.
?

He was so excited, he _____ to grab his daughter,
→

Zoe, to tell her the _____ news. As
😊

soon as they touched, she became a golden statue.

King Midas _____ collapsed
?

on the floor in tears. "What a fool I have been,"

he cried. "I wish I had never wished."

PHONICS AND WORD STUDY

Final Stable Syllables

Some **syllables** are common at the ends of words.
Looking for these syllables can help you chunk and read longer words.

Consonant + le	Other
bat/**tle**	lo/**tion**
fa/**ble**	mis/**sion**
han/**dle**	cap/**ture**
gig/**gle**	pres/**sure**

Add the missing **final syllable**.

poo __ __ __

televi __ __ __ __

ea __ __ __

erup __ __ __ __

bot __ __ __

pic __ __ __ __

puz __ __ __

trea __ __ __ __

NOUN	VERB	ADJECTIVE	ADVERB
★	➡	☺	?
barns	slither	brave	easily
homes	dance	pink	hungrily
castles	wiggle	noble	wildly
restaurants	sleep	sneezy	timidly

My Television or Yours?

A television is a common fixture in most _____ and
★

_____ . You can see adventure shows about _____
★   ☺

explorers finding new places and things in the middle of nowhere. You can learn about

unusual creatures that _____ in faraway places. You can see fiction
➡

books turned into _____ movies, and so much more. It's a pleasure
☺

to spend your leisure time in front of a television. But what will the future hold for TV?

Will we _____ as scientists _____
➡   ?

capture Bigfoot or the Loch Ness Monster? Will new shows

be about us and our _____
☺

lives? Only time will tell!

Using Prefixes to Sound Out Words

A **prefix** is a word part added to the beginning of a word, such as **un** and **re**.

Quickly seeing these common word parts can help you chunk and read longer words.

unhappy   **re**write   **dis**agree   **mis**use

Circle the **prefix** in each word.

undo   reread   dislike

precook   misread   midafternoon

rewrapped   disobey   unpacking

NOUN ★	VERB →	ADJECTIVE 😀	ADVERB ?
home	precooked	spotted	often
zoo	preplanned	zippy	rarely
bathroom	preordered	dirty	never
treehouse	prewashed	laughing	sometimes

Oops!

It was a rather unsuccessful and unhappy week. But who could have predicted how much I'd learn from my mistakes? Let me tell you about them.

1. At my _____ ★ , I _____ → my lunch. But when I grabbed it, I uncovered the truth. A _____ 😀 zebra had eaten it.

2. I misread the directions for making my cake. Sadly, I _____ ? do. It looked like a _____ 😀 turtle.

3. I dislike cleaning my private _____ ★ , but I refuse to live in a mess. Hours later, I found a _____ 😀 lion drooling on the floor. Ugh!

What did I learn from my terrible week? I can't wait for next week!

Using Suffixes to Sound Out Words

A **suffix** is a word part added to the end of a word, such as **ed** and **ful**.
Quickly seeing these common word parts can help you chunk and read longer words.

plant**ed**   use**ful**   hope**less**

Circle the **suffix** or **suffixes** in each word.

sending   useless   stranded

ordered   suddenly   carelessness

darkness   beautifully   helpful

NOUN ★	VERB ➡	ADJECTIVE 😊	ADVERB ?
mushrooms	running	inner	suddenly
monsters	screaming	whistling	accidentally
caves	passing out	endless	annoyingly
coconuts	panicking	volcanic	almost

Helpful or Not?

Luis and Pablo are debating whether or not to take their phone on their camping trip.

Luis: I think a phone is helpful. What if you _____ get stuck in
                                                            ?

the darkness of the _____ forest? You can search for directions.
                            😊

You can call for help. And if a bear attacks you, you can quickly look up what to do

(while you're _____).
                    ➡

Pablo: I think a phone is useless in the _____ forest. You
                                              😊

should be enjoying the quiet and looking for _____ and
                                                          ★

_____ . A camping trip is all
        ★

about relaxing and appreciating nature. Not

_____ . A phone is a distraction.
        ➡

What do you think? Helpful or not?

Reading Words with Latin Suffixes

A **suffix** is a word part added to the end of a word.

Some suffixes, such as **able**, **ible**, **ation**, **ment**, **ty**, and **ity**, come from Latin.

That's a language that was spoken long ago.

Noun	Adjective
cre**ation**	siz**able**
state**ment**	flex**ible**
certain**ty**	
similar**ity**	

Add the **suffix** to each word to make a new word. Sometimes the spelling changes. Sometimes the pronunciation changes, too.

inform + ation = _____

loyal + ty = _____

govern + ment = _____

like + able = _____

amaze + ment = _____

electric + ity = _____

comfort + able = _____

reverse + ible = _____

NOUN	VERB	ADJECTIVE	ADVERB
★	➡	😀	?
juice	sob	horrible	bravely
pickles	squabble	unbelievable	loudly
tacos	wobble	breezy	softly
candy	flee	goofy	cheerfully

The Royal Court

The kingdom of Ooh-la-la was a peaceful place until one _____

😀

day in December. The king, the queen, and their royal court entered the palace.

A soldier on horseback _____ raced into the main room.

?

"I have terrible information," he shouted. "We are about to be attacked. It's just

_____." "I thought we were the most likable kingdom in

😀

the world," said the king. "All we ask is for our subjects to give us loyalty,

kindness, and _____," said the queen. "We will not fight,

★

_____, or act with cruelty. We will

➡

_____ offer our attackers

?

entertainment and _____ . Why?

★

We are a peaceable place."

Chunking Big Words to Read Them

When you see a long word while reading, chunk it into smaller parts to sound it out.

If the word has two consonants in the middle, such as **middle**, divide the word between the two consonants: **mid/dle**.

<u>nap</u>/<u>kin</u>   <u>les</u>/<u>son</u>

Write the two parts of each word.

puddle   _____   _____

rubber   _____   _____

magnet   _____   _____

cactus   _____   _____

public   _____   _____

Think of words you know with two syllables or word parts.
Write them in smaller chunks.

1. _____   _____

2. _____   _____

3. _____   _____

NOUN ★	VERB ➡	ADJECTIVE 😊	ADVERB ?
blanket	juggle	silly	quietly
napkin	giggle	funny	loudly
log	tumble	purple	secretly
bush	fiddle	little	surprisingly

Turtle and Rabbit

You've all heard the famous story "The Tortoise and the Hare." But have you ever read

"The Turtle and the Rabbit"? It's a tale about two animals, similar to the original tale,

but with different ways of running in a _____ race. The turtle prided
😊

herself on being _____ and able to _____ better
😊   ➡

than any other animal. The rabbit prided himself on being _____
😊

and able to _____ better than any other animal. So, during the
➡

race, the turtle _____ slept on a _____ .
?   ★

The rabbit _____ napped under a
?

_____ . As a result, the race never
★

ended. And that's why no one knows this story!

Reading Big Words Strategy

When you see a long word while reading, use these five steps to chunk it into smaller parts to read it.

Step 1: Look for common word parts at the beginning, such as prefixes (**un**, **re**, **dis**, **mis**).

Step 2: Look for common word parts at the end, such as suffixes (**ing**, **ed**, **ful**, **less**).

Step 3: Look at what's left. Use what you know about sounding out words and syllable types to chunk it.

Step 4: Sound out all the word parts slowly. It will be close to the real word.

Step 5: Say the word parts fast. Adjust your pronunciation to say it correctly.

Check the steps you use to figure out these words. Write the meaning of each word.

rereading

☐ Step 1

☐ Step 2

☐ Step 3

☐ Step 4

☐ Step 5

Meaning: _____

_____

_____

unhelpful

☐ Step 1

☐ Step 2

☐ Step 3

☐ Step 4

☐ Step 5

Meaning: _____

_____

_____

NOUN ★	VERB →	ADJECTIVE 😊	ADVERB ?
wheat	fiddling	tiny	softly
beetles	dancing	overflowing	angrily
soup	leaping	wooden	gently
berries	singing	sparkly	harshly

The Ants and the Grasshopper

Winter was fast approaching. The ants busied themselves preparing for the cold days

and nights. They gathered _____ and _____ ★ ★

and precooked the _____ ★ to store in their _____ 😊

cupboards. But the grasshopper spent his days _____ → and

_____ → in the fields. As the icy winds blew and the snow tumbled

from the skies, the grasshopper could find no food. He _____ ?

knocked on the ants' door. "Why are you so unprepared?" they asked. "Rethink your

preparation next year...if you survive!" And with that, they _____ ?

closed the door.

There's a time for work and a time for play.

Read Irregularly Spelled Words

Most words in English can be sounded out using what you know about common letters, spellings, and sounds. However, there are some words that don't follow the rules. These words need special attention. Follow these steps to learn these words.

Step 1: Read the word. Say the sounds you hear in it.

Step 2: Spell the word out loud.

Step 3: Write the word as you say the letter names.

Use the three steps to practice the words below. Check the box after completing Steps 1 and 2. Write the word for Step 3.

was	Step 1 ☐	Step 2 ☐	Step 3 _____
one	Step 1 ☐	Step 2 ☐	Step 3 _____
there	Step 1 ☐	Step 2 ☐	Step 3 _____
where	Step 1 ☐	Step 2 ☐	Step 3 _____
come	Step 1 ☐	Step 2 ☐	Step 3 _____
some	Step 1 ☐	Step 2 ☐	Step 3 _____
would	Step 1 ☐	Step 2 ☐	Step 3 _____
should	Step 1 ☐	Step 2 ☐	Step 3 _____
give	Step 1 ☐	Step 2 ☐	Step 3 _____
have	Step 1 ☐	Step 2 ☐	Step 3 _____

NOUN	VERB	ADJECTIVE	ADVERB
★	→	☺	?
monster	ice-skate	lazy	sadly
cookie	fly	sleepy	unfortunately
worm	boogie	chubby	predictably
giraffe	twirl	hungry	obviously

Once Upon a Time

Once upon a time, there was a giant _____ .
                ★

Some people said he could _____ and
             →

_____ really well. Others said he was too
    →

_____ to do anything but eat. They were all
   ☺

wrong! "I have an idea," squawked the giant. "I will give gifts to all

the village children. But where will I find some good ones?" The giant

looked here, there, and everywhere. _____ , he found none.
                ?

So, he _____ returned home to do the one thing he loved
    ?

most: _____ .
    →

Inflectional Endings with Spelling Changes

When you add **s**, **es**, **ed**, or **ing** to a word, you sometimes have to change the spelling before adding the ending.

1. Double the final consonant

| stop | stops | sto**pp**ed | sto**pp**ing |

2. Drop e

| save | saves | sav**ed** | sav**ing** |

3. Change y to i

| cry | cr**i**es | cr**i**ed | crying |

Add **s**, **ed**, and **ing** to each word.

	Add **s** or **es**	Add **ed**	Add **ing**
tap	_____	_____	_____
bake	_____	_____	_____
reply	_____	_____	_____

NOUN	VERB	ADJECTIVE	ADVERB
★	→	😀	?
bush	smelled	nervous	usually
bus station	grabbed	timid	always
toilet	stole	attractive	generally
garbage can	borrowed	unlikely	typically

The Spy That Cries

Spies in movies are _____ brave, clever, and heroic. But once, there
                                                    ?

was a/an _____ spy who could do nothing but cry. People called
                              😀

him the "Spy That Cries." And no matter how hard he tried, all he did was cry.

One day, the spy was hiding in a _____ . He spotted a thief in
                                                    ★

a _____ making his evil move. Instead of stopping the bandit,
              ★

the spy went shopping. He _____ gloves and
                                              →

_____ a purse for his grandmother. No
              →

saving the day here! As a result, he got fired. And do

you know what? That really made him cry!

YOU'RE FIRED

WRITING: Spelling, Grammar, and Story Structure

Spelling Multisyllabic Words

When spelling a longer word, it is easier to chunk it into smaller parts or syllables. Then spell each part, one at a time. Think about other words you know with these same or similar parts.

Break each word into syllables. Write each syllable in the blanks.

railroad   _____   _____

misreading   _____   _____   _____

independence   _____   _____   _____   _____

unexpected   _____   _____   _____   _____

Look at each picture. Say the picture name. Write each word part by part (syllable by syllable).

_____   _____

_____   _____   _____

_____   _____   _____

_____   _____   _____   _____

NOUN ★	VERB →	ADJECTIVE 😊	ADVERB ?
superhero	twists	tiny	Happily
fall leaf	dances	woolly	Suddenly
hatched bird	wiggles	chubby	Beautifully
burned log	snoozes	cute	Wonderfully

On Becoming a Butterfly

The life cycle of a butterfly is one of extraordinary change. It's a spectacular

metamorphosis. It begins with a _____ caterpillar crawling on a
(adjective)

_____ twig and munching on leaves. Then the time comes. The
(adjective)

caterpillar spins a chrysalis and _____ and _____
(verb) _(verb)_

inside. Time passes. Inside, something changes, and this new creature begins to

emerge from the hard shell. A head pokes out. Then wings. _____,
(adverb)

out flutters a beautiful butterfly. Like a _____
(noun)

or a _____, the change is complete.
(noun)

Abracadabra! It's the magic of nature.

WRITING: Spelling, Grammar, and Story Structure

Irregular Plural Nouns

A **plural** word is more than one of something.
Most naming words, or nouns, add **s** or **es** to make it plural.
However, some plural words do not. We call them irregular.

Regular

1 train   2 train**s**   1 box   2 box**es**

Irregular

1 woman   2 women   1 mouse   2 mice

Write the **plural** of each word.

1 foot   2 _____   1 man   2 _____

1 goose   2 _____   1 person   2 _____

1 knife   2 _____   1 child   2 _____

1 tooth   2 _____   1 sheep   2 _____

NOUN	VERB	ADJECTIVE	ADVERB
★	→	☺	?
pinstripes	moo	sharp	easily
purses	sew	dirty	surprisingly
goggles	cook	silver	occasionally
knives	cuddle	rubber	often

Keeper of the Sheep

Each year, people flock to visit the local sheep farm. At the

farm, they can _____ view
?

sheep with _____ teeth,
☺

porcupines with _____
☺

_____ , and cows that
★

_____ . Men and women gather to
→

take photographs of the mice that can _____ and the geese with
→

_____ that squawk loudly. These people can also take their children
★

to nibble on treats made by the farmer that are _____ the best food
?

in the area. This all makes a trip to the country a special adventure!

Pronoun-Antecedent Agreement

A **pronoun** is a word that takes the place of a noun. Words like **he**, **she**, **it**, and **they** are pronouns.

Writers use pronouns to avoid saying the noun over and over. It makes their writing more interesting.

An **antecedent** is the word the pronoun refers to. For example, read the sentences below. The pronoun is **it** and **dog** is the antecedent. The word **it** takes the place of the noun **dog**.

> The <u>dog</u> is fluffy. <u>It</u> is also black.

A **singular** (meaning "one") **pronoun** takes the place of a singular noun. Singular pronouns include **he**, **she**, **you**, and **it**.

A **plural** (meaning "more than one") **pronoun** takes the place of a plural noun. Plural pronouns include **we** and **they**.

Add the correct **pronoun**.

1. The man wears a black suit with a purple tie. _____ is very tall.

2. My sister and I bought a microwave for our mother. _____ got it on sale.

3. Mrs. Chen is a great storyteller. _____ told us a traditional tale from China.

4. The dog leaped into air. _____ looked like a superhero.

5. The children played soccer at recess. _____ had tons of fun!

NOUN	VERB	ADJECTIVE	ADVERB
★	➡	☺	?
raccoon	swim	rambunctious	quite
hippo	bathe	happy	very
mosquito	relax	mini	entirely
panda	juggle	pretty	enormously

The Family Called Strange

New neighbors just moved in. And let me tell you something—they are

strange. Yes, that's right. Their last name is Strange. Grandpa Strange likes to

_____ in the nearby lake each morning. He is in great physical shape!
➡

Grandma Strange likes to walk her _____ _____
☺ ★

in the afternoon after a healthy lunch. She sings as she walks. Papa and Mama Strange

like to _____ in the evenings before dinner. They seem so happy.
➡

Then there is Baby Strange and her _____ pet
☺

_____ . She hugs and cuddles it all day. We love
★

our new neighbors, and they are _____ thrilled to
?

live in our neighborhood!

Adjectives

An **adjective** is a describing word. It tells more about something.

a bear

a **little** **black** bear

a **big** **angry** bear

Add **adjectives** to finish each sentence.

1. The _____ stars lit up the night sky like diamonds.

2. My dog Scruffles is _____ and _____ .

3. The _____ giraffe nibbled on the _____

leaves at the top of the tree.

4. When I see a _____ insect, I run the other way!

5. A _____ movie is my favorite, but I don't enjoy

_____ ones.

6. The _____ _____ children raced

through the hallways.

7. My coat was _____ , but now it's old and

_____ .

NOUN ★	VERB →	ADJECTIVE ☺	ADVERB ?
crocodile	screech	delicate	magically
beagle	bite	bony	gently
dinosaur	bend	beautiful	quickly
doctor	twirl	daring	hurriedly

Is This a Poem?

My teacher, Mr. Hernandez, asked us to write an interesting poem for homework. But I

wasn't sure how. I had read some poems that rhyme, so I wrote:

Watch a _____ butterfly as it flutter-flies by.
      ☺

Watch a _____ _____ ask why, oh, why?
      ☺   ★

Watch a _____ cry and eat some pecan pie.
      ★

But this sounded like something my little sister would write—silly. So, I decided to

stop rhyming and be what Mr. Hernandez calls "descriptive and lyrical." I wrote:

On a cold night,

Winds _____ and trees _____
         →   →

As children _____ huddle.
               ?

Winter _____ approaches.
          ?

What do you think? Is this really a poem?

Adverbs

An **adverb** is a word that tells more about a verb.
It can tell how, when, or where.

We shouted **loudly**.	(how)
We went to a restaurant **yesterday**.	(when)
We played soccer **outside**.	(where)

Adverbs that compare two things end in **er** or add **more**.
José worked **harder** than his big brother.
Marko ran **more slowly** than his best friend.

Adverbs that compare three or more things end in **est** or add **most**.
Martina ran the **fastest** of all her classmates.
That was the **most quietly** we ever watched TV.

Add one of these **adverbs** to finish each sentence:
slower, fastest, more loudly, most joyfully.

1. Tomás shouted _____ than his sister Graciela.

2. Is a turtle _____ than a frog?

3. A cheetah is the _____ animal I have ever seen!

4. We sang the _____ of all the holiday choirs.

NOUN	VERB	ADJECTIVE	ADVERB
★	→	☺	?
slime	dance	purple	crazier
goop	wiggle	glowing	funnier
chickens	bounce	bubbly	sillier
juice	sleep	ticklish	wilder

The Contest

Once, Elephant and Crocodile had a contest. "I am _____ [?] than

you," announced Elephant. "I will pour _____ [★] on my head and

_____ [→] on this wobbly chair." Crocodile snorted. "I will roll in

_____ [★] and boogie on this bed!" "I am _____ [?]

than you," Elephant shouted back. "I will _____ [→] and fall on

this _____ [☺] table." "I'm the craziest!" laughed Crocodile. "I can

juggle a _____ [☺] clown!" "I'm the funniest!" Elephant demanded.

"I know the most jokes in all the world!" Then Anteater arrived. "Neither of you are

_____ [?] than me. I am the greatest!" "And

clearly the most humble," said Elephant and Crocodile as they

turned and walked away.

Abstract Nouns

Most nouns are things you can see, like **baby**, **butterfly**, or **balloon**. However, some nouns you can't see, hear, taste, touch, or smell. We call these **abstract nouns**. They stand for concepts like **freedom** and **curiosity**.

Complete each sentence with one of these **abstract nouns**: **ability**, **appetite**, **bravery**, **friendship**, **goal**, **kindness**, **success**.

1. She has the _____ to sing and tumble at the same time!

2. My _____ with my sister is very important to me.

3. The firefighters' _____ helped to save the family from the blaze.

4. He showed great _____ when he helped the elderly lady cross the street.

5. Our _____ in winning the competition depends on hard work and skill.

6. My _____ is to become a doctor someday.

7. Whenever I smell pizza, my _____ seems to grow bigger!

NOUN	VERB	ADJECTIVE	ADVERB
★	→	☺	?
friendship	twitch	sunny	awkwardly
love	scratch	rainy	cheerfully
hope	scream	cloudy	glumly
bravery	snore	stormy	lazily

Rainy Day Blues

Can bad weather cause bad moods? Research has shown that weather can affect

people's feelings and thoughts. This is certainly true in my family. For example,

overcast days make my grandpa gloomily wonder about _____ .
                                                            ★

My brother feels scared when it thunders, but snowy days make him sing

_____ . On _____ days, my mom hollers about
         ?   ☺

giving us too much freedom. Once, a hurricane made my aunt _____
                                                                      →

and yell so _____ , the dog hid under the bed. Since yesterday
                   ?

was _____ , my sister mumbled about _____ .
          ☺   ★

Today is _____ , so I'll probably just
              ☺

stay in bed!

Conjunctions

A **conjunction** is a word that connects (or joins) words, parts of sentences, and sentences. Think of them as glue words. You can remember the seven main conjunctions by remembering this:

FANBOYS

For   The goat must have been very hungry, **for** she gobbled her food.

And   We play soccer **and** volleyball at school.

Nor   Neither my mom **nor** my dad drink tomato juice.

But   After the race, I felt tired **but** happy.

Or   Do you want pepperoni **or** olives on your pizza?

Yet   It was early, **yet** we all wanted to eat dinner.

So   I am tired, **so** I think I'll skip that TV show tonight.

Add a **conjunction** to complete each sentence.

1. We will eat hamburgers _____ hot dogs at our cookout.

2. Do you prefer summer _____ winter?

3. My dog ate a big bowl of food, _____ still

   seemed hungry.

4. Neither my sister _____ I have green eyes like

   our mother.

5. I have tons of homework, _____

   I will have to focus to finish it.

NOUN ★	VERB ➡	ADJECTIVE 😊	ADVERB ?
cattle	ate	serious	cheerily
rats	painted	boring	quietly
arrows	flipped	clever	loudly
socks	cooked	dizzy	sweetly

Hermes the Trickster

Long ago, two brothers named Hermes and Apollo lived in ancient Greece. The

brothers were gods and had special powers, yet they were very different. Hermes was

a trickster, so one day he _____ Apollo's _____ .
                              ➡   ★

Hermes hid behind a tree and laughed _____ as he waited for
                                              ?

his _____ brother Apollo to arrive. "Do you honestly believe you
        😊

should do this _____ crime?" Apollo cried. "Stop tricking me
                      😊

or else!" But Hermes continued to laugh _____ . Then he
                                                  ?

_____ Apollo's _____ .
        ➡   ★

"Oh, my _____ brother," Hermes
                😊

said. "I am truly trying to stop, but I'm way

too tricky!"

Irregular Past Tense Verbs

Most **past tense verbs** end in **ed**.

Today, I **walk** to the store.   (present)

Last week, I **walked** to the store.   (past)

However, some verbs do not. We call these irregular.

Today, I **drink** orange juice.   (present)

Yesterday, I **drank** a glass of milk. (past)

Finish each sentence with the **past tense** form of each verb.

1. (buy)   Yesterday, I _____ a new notebook for school.

2. (build)   Last year, they _____ a new mall in our town.

3. (leave)   Yesterday, she _____ that package for you.

4. (catch)   Last week, I _____ a very bad cold.

5. (spend)   Yesterday, I _____ twenty dollars on a new shirt.

6. (hear)   One time, I _____ a strange noise in the attic.

NOUN	VERB	ADJECTIVE	ADVERB
★	➡	😀	?
insects	dove	fiery	totally
sludge	flew	cozy	really
bats	drove	fuzzy	surprisingly
fish	froze	freezing	frankly

The Monster Party

My new neighbor invited me to her party. I was nervous because she was a monster—a

real monster! But I went because I didn't want to be rude. First, all the monsters and I

_____ in the swimming pool. The water was _____
    ➡   😀

and full of _____ , which _____ freaked me out.
             ★   ?

Then we all crawled into a _____ cave and _____
                         😀   ➡

until we couldn't speak. After that, we ate bright green birthday cake. Finally,

a band of lizards _____ in the room, and it
                     ➡

was _____ awesome. I'm really
      ?

glad I went to that party!

Subject-Verb Agreement

The **subject** and **verb** of a sentence must both be singular (showing one) or both be plural (showing more than one). They must "agree."

The **elephant stomps** through the mud.
(elephant = one elephant = singular)
(stomps, as in "it stomps" = singular)

The **elephants stomp** through the mud.
(elephants = more than one elephant = plural)
(stomp, as in "they stomp" = plural)

Write the **verb** that best fits each sentence. Make sure the subject and the verb "agree."

1. The dog _____ his food. (gobble/gobbles)

2. We _____ around the playground. (race/races)

3. The children _____ to watch the movie. (gather/gathers)

4. Mom and Dad _____ at the market on Saturdays.

   (shop/shops)

5. When a volcano _____ , it spews lava. (explode/explodes)

6. Those cars _____ on electricity. (run/runs)

7. Pencils _____ my favorite writing tool. (is/are)

NOUN	VERB	ADJECTIVE	ADVERB
★	➡	😊	?
thieves	invite	angry	always
pests	attract	creepy	loosely
monsters	eat	happy	nervously
bugs	love	weird	happily

Bats to the Rescue

Do you think bats are _____ ? If so, you are not alone. Most people
<small>😊</small>

are afraid of these _____ creatures. After all, a bat is neither cute nor
<small>😊</small>

cuddly. However, this strange-looking mammal does important work for our farmers.

Most farmers are _____ satisfied when bats live near their farms.
<small>?</small>

They _____ this unusual animal! Why? Bats are nocturnal, and they
<small>➡</small>

_____ insects that come out at night. If bats weren't around, these
<small>➡</small>

pesky _____ would eat all the crops!
<small>★</small>

Some farmers build bat homes because they want to

_____ bats. They _____
<small>➡</small>   <small>?</small>

hang these houses in their barns. Every smart farmer

knows that bats make good neighbors.

Compound Sentences

A **compound sentence** has two sentences put together.
The words **and**, **but**, **or**, and **so** are used to make a compound sentence.
A comma (**,**) is put before one of these words.

> Mark played soccer**, and** I read a book.
> I like to sleep late**, but** I have to get up early tomorrow.

Put together the two sentences to make a **compound sentence**.

I play soccer. My brother plays basketball.

_____

We like to eat candy. Our school doesn't allow it.

_____

Complex Sentences

A **complex sentence** has an **independent clause** (a complete sentence) and a **dependent clause** (not a complete sentence and cannot stand on its own). The **dependent clause** begins with a word like **after**, **although**, **as**, **because**, **before**, **even**, **though**, **unless**, **whenever**, and **wherever**.

> Our democracy works | because people have the right to vote.
> ‾‾‾‾‾‾‾‾‾‾‾‾‾‾‾‾‾‾‾‾‾‾ ‾‾‾‾‾‾‾‾‾‾‾‾‾‾‾‾‾‾‾‾‾‾‾‾‾‾‾‾‾‾‾‾‾‾
> **independent clause**   **dependent clause**

Add a **dependent clause** to make a **complex sentence**.

I want to go home _____

_____.

NOUN	VERB	ADJECTIVE	ADVERB
★	➡	😊	?
attic	looked	cheerful	nicely
bathroom	hopped	adorable	comfortably
basement	skipped	miserable	tightly
dishwasher	jumped	frantic	softly

Where Is Buster?

Buster had been missing since noon, and Emma was _____ .
                                                            😊

She figured out that she probably hadn't closed the cage door of his cozy pen

_____ . That's how Buster _____ out, and it
       ?   ➡

was all her fault! Meanwhile, Emma had _____ everywhere for
                                              ➡

her pet rabbit, including the backyard, the garage, and the _____ .
                                                                    ★

She had even looked in the _____ , but no Buster! Now Emma was
                                  ★

sitting on the porch, worrying that she might never see her _____
                                                                    😊

pet again. Suddenly, she thought of one more place to search. Emma

_____ down and peered below the raised
       ➡

porch. Sure enough, there was Buster, resting

_____ in the dark.
       ?

Possessives

A **possessive noun** shows who or what owns something. Add **'s** to a noun that names one thing (singular noun).

> This is the grizzly **bear's** cave.

Add just an **'** to a noun that names more than one thing, and ends in **s** (plural noun).

> The three **boys'** rooms are filled with books.

If a plural noun does NOT end in **s**, add **'s**.

> The **men's** team rode the bus to the game.

Fix each sentence.

1. The scientists found a dinosaur_____ bones.

2. All four dogs_____ food was kept under the sink.

3. The women_____ hats were on sale.

4. The children_____ games are kept in the closet.

5. My mom_____ favorite cake is chocolate with strawberries.

6. The school_____ principal greets the students each morning.

NOUN	VERB	ADJECTIVE	ADVERB
★	➡	😊	?
clowns	sweeping	strange	extremely
critters	munching	goofy	pretty
chickens	baking	wild	totally
dentists	splashing	silly	really

Winter Fun

Dear Alex,

I miss you a lot since you moved to Florida. Our new neighbors, the Nelsons, are

_____ nice _____ , but things aren't the
         ?   **★**

same without you! Thanks for your email with your mom's pictures of you

_____ in the ocean. I admit I'm _____ jealous
         ➡   **?**

because it's freezing here in Chicago. But chilly weather can be fun. I'm attaching

some photos to remind you! Here I am, _____ a snowman in the
                                                  ➡

Nelsons' yard (your yard!). The snowman's _____
                                                      😊

hat belongs to my dad, and his _____ scarf
                                        😊

is Mr. Nelson's. Write soon about your neighbors, the loud

_____ . —Abby
         ★

Capitalization

What begins with a **capital letter**?

- the first word in a sentence
- the word **I**
- the name and title of a specific person
- the title of a book

>My favorite book is **_Wonder_**.
>
>**Dr. Jackson** is giving out free flu shots this week.
>
>**Mrs. Ling**, our teacher, read **Harry Potter** to us.

Fix each sentence.

1. my class is reading a biography called *spotted tail.*

_____

2. does mr. sanchez own the new cupcake business in town?

_____

3. *stuart little* is a book about a mouse.

_____

4. i just finished reading *charlotte's web* and cried.

_____

5. i hope gov. mitchum will visit our school.

_____

NOUN ★	VERB ➡	ADJECTIVE 😊	ADVERB ?
turkeys	drawing	grumpy	absolutely
giants	writing	wacky	always
meatballs	eating	silly	truly
copycats	buying	clever	clearly

Happy Birthday, Dr. Seuss!

Each year on March 2, students and _____ celebrate Read Across
★

America Day. That date is the birthday of the _____ children's
😊

book author Dr. Seuss. As you _____ know, millions of kids
?

learned how to read using his _____ books, like *The Cat in the*
😊

Hat and *Green* _____ *and Ham.* Of course,
★

Dr. Seuss wasn't _____ a doctor. His real
?

name was Mr. Theodor Seuss Geisel. Early in his career,

he worked as an illustrator for _____
😊

magazines. Then, luckily for kids everywhere, he began

_____ children's books. Dr. Seuss ended
➡

up _____ more than sixty books!
➡

Commas in Quotations

Use a **comma** to separate a direct quote and who is saying it. The comma appears **before** the quotation mark (").

> "I am running late for school," said Daniel.
> My mother yelled, "Hurry up!"

Add the missing **comma** in each sentence.

1. "Please help me " said the boy.

2. "I really want to play soccer today " said Juan Carlos.

3. The mouse ran from the owl, screeching "Eek!"

4. Li said "My favorite movies are action films."

Commas in Addresses

Use a **comma** in an address to separate the city from the state.

> Lupé Lopez
> 12 East 34th Street
> Springfield, AZ 56789

Write a school's address below.

_____

_____

_____

NOUN	VERB	ADJECTIVE	ADVERB
★	➡	😊	?
pillow	bouncing	nasty	backward
mustache	hopping	rotten	sideways
poem	skipping	foolish	downstairs
bed	strutting	scrumptious	underground

The Fox and the Crow

One morning, a crow was looking for food. Suddenly, he saw a _____ (😊)

piece of cheese. "I am very hungry," he thought. "This cheese will make a

delicious _____ (★)!" The crow picked up the cheese and flew

_____ (?) to a branch. At the same time, a fox was

_____ (➡) by. He wanted the cheese and came up with

an idea. "I've heard you have a fine _____ (★)," said

the fox. "Won't you sing for me, too?" The crow wanted to show

off his voice and began _____ (➡). As he did, the cheese

fell _____ (?). "I am very clever," thought the fox as he

went _____ (➡) off with the cheese.

Quotes

Use **quotation marks** when quoting the exact words someone says.

"I will be late to the party," said Dr. Velazquez.
The giant screamed, "Fee, fi, fo, fum!"

Add the missing **quotation marks** in each sentence.

1. I hope we order pizza after the game, said the boy.

2. We can shop at the mall tomorrow, said Mom.

3. What are you reading this week? asked Mrs. Jung.

4. Help! Help! shouted the man. My house is on fire!

Write sentences showing a conversation between you and a friend or family member.

1. _____

2. _____

3. _____

4. _____

NOUN ★	VERB →	ADJECTIVE 😊	ADVERB ?
chef	pretend	nasty	never
dancer	boast	jolly	sometimes
juggler	giggle	wacky	always
detective	fight	clever	rarely

A Man of Many Talents

Ben Franklin was a scientist, an inventor, and a _____ ★ . He was

also one of our country's founders and helped write the Declaration of Independence.

Ben attended school for only a few years. His family was poor, and he had to

_____ → to help them. However, he _____ ? loved

to read and _____ → . As a young man, he moved to Philadelphia

and started a newspaper. He also wrote a popular almanac that included

_____ 😊 and interesting sayings, for example:

"A true _____ ★ is the best possession," and

"No gains without pains." Today we _____ ?

appreciate these sayings, or proverbs, which are

still _____ 😊 and _____ 😊 .

Text Structure: Sequence

Writers of informational text use different ways to **structure** their writing. One way is to put the information in **sequence**, or **time order**.

These signal words often alert a reader that the text is organized this way: **first, second, third, next, then, last, after, finally, before, in the beginning, to start, meanwhile, in the middle, at the end**. The writer might also use **dates in order (such as 1776, 1865, and 2020)**.

Fill in the **sequence** paragraph. Write about an interesting topic, like cooking something or making a craft.

The **first** step in making _____ is to _____

_____ .

After that, you must _____

_____ .

Next, you need to _____

_____ .

Finally, you _____

_____ .

The Changing Leaves

NOUN ★: breakfast, dinner, soup, pancakes

VERB →: twirl, toss, break, kick

ADJECTIVE ☺: ugly, enormous, purple, smelly

ADVERB ?: magically, wonderfully, mysteriously, tragically

If you live in certain parts of the country, you get to see the leaves _____ (?) _____ (→) with each season. In summer, the leaves are a deep green color. The green leaves make _____ (★) for the tree. In autumn, the leaves _____ (→) their green color and stop making _____ (★). Now they are orange, red, yellow, and _____ (☺). When winter arrives, the leaves die and fall _____ (?) from the tree. However, the roots, trunk, and branches are _____ (☺) enough to survive the cold. Finally, when spring comes, the air gets warmer. Warm air and sunlight help the tree grow _____ (☺) leaves. Soon the branches are covered with pale green leaves.

Text Structure: Cause/Effect

Writers of informational text use different ways to **structure** their writing. One way is to explain the **causes** and **effects** of something. The causes are **why** something happens. The effects are **what** happens.

These signal words often alert a reader that the text is organized this way: **because, cause, effect, therefore, if...then, as a result, due to, reason, since, leads to, as a consequence, consequently**.

Fill in the **cause and effect** paragraph. Write about an interesting topic, like climate change or invasive animals attacking plants and animals in an environment.

Because of _____ , _____

_____

_____ has happened.

Therefore, _____

_____

_____.

This explains why _____

_____

_____.

NOUN ★	VERB →	ADJECTIVE ☺	ADVERB ?
whiskers	hate	hairy	quickly
toes	please	chubby	carefully
ears	forget	messy	sloppily
food	spoil	flabby	frequently

Healthy and Happy Pets

Pets need our help. Animal experts report that more than half of our cats and dogs are

overweight. Why are they so _____ (☺) ? The reason is simple. We feed them

too _____ (?) ! _____ (☺) pets are at risk for health problems,

like heart disease. These problems can prevent pets from leading _____ (☺)

lives. What should owners do if their pets are too _____ (☺) ? Give them

smaller portions and don't feed them as _____ (?) . Regular exercise is

important, too. Many owners _____ (→) their pets by giving

them human _____ (★) . Experts say that pets

should only eat their own _____ (★) . If owners

wish to _____ (→) their pets, they should play

with them. This results in happy, healthy pets!

VOCABULARY

Prefixes

A **prefix** is a word part added to the beginning of a word.
It changes the meaning of the word.

un, **in** = not, the opposite of

re = again

happy	**un**happy	(not happy)
visible	**in**visible	(not visible)
read	**re**read	(read again)

Add **un**, **in**, or **re** to finish each word.

_____make   _____able

_____friendly   _____appear

_____correct   _____ability

_____try   _____do

_____even   _____complete

NOUN ★	VERB →	ADJECTIVE ☺	ADVERB ?
creep	sniffed	lumpy	noisily
skunk	squeezed	slimy	badly
bandit	scrubbed	mushy	awkwardly
beast	destroyed	teeny	sleepily

Carrot Thief

An unknown thief had stolen carrots from Rose's garden. Who could this

invisible _____ ★ be? Rose was confident that she could solve

the crime and find the _____ ★ ! She reviewed the crime scene

_____ ? . She would not overlook any clues. Rose saw that the gate was

locked, so maybe a tall _____ ★ had climbed over it. Or perhaps

a small _____ ★ had crawled under it. The carrots were gone, but

the rest of the garden was untouched. Then she _____ → some

_____ ☺ footprints. Rose _____ ? retraced them to

the edge of the woods, where they stopped at a _____ ☺

rabbit hole. She had solved the crime! Case closed.

Prefixes

A **prefix** is a word part added to the beginning of a word. It changes the meaning of the word.

dis, **il** = not, the opposite of
mis = bad, wrong, incorrectly

like	**dis**like	(the opposite of like)
treat	**mis**treat	(treat badly or wrongly)
logical	**il**logical	(not logical)

Add **dis**, **mis**, or **il** to finish each word.

_____agree   _____legal

_____obey   _____able

_____understood   _____appear

_____order   _____legible

_____lead   _____place

_____heard   _____trust

_____judge   _____literate

_____honest   _____print

NOUN ★	VERB ➡	ADJECTIVE 😊	ADVERB ?
lights	misplace	ridiculous	happily
brains	waste	dishonest	sadly
relatives	lose	sweaty	correctly
lamps	ruin	productive	slowly

Screen-Free Week

Each year, during the first week of May, people everywhere try to disconnect from their

TVs, computers, _____ , and _____ . The goal
                          ★   ★

of Screen-Free Week isn't about giving up technology _____ .
                                                              ?

It's all about learning to be more _____ about how we
                                            😊

_____ our time. When people turn off their _____ ,
        ➡   ★

they can _____ reconnect to other activities. Many health experts
                  ?

warn that people are misusing technology. Too much screen time leads to an inactive

lifestyle, which is very unhealthy. When people _____
                                                        ➡

their devices, they rediscover other _____ ways to
                                              😊

enjoy themselves. So, think about it. If you give up some screen time,

what else could you _____ ?
                            ➡

Suffixes

A **suffix** is a word part added to the end of a word.
It changes the meaning of the word.

ful = full of, with
less = without, not

fear	fear**ful**	(full of fear)
hope	hope**less**	(without hope)

Add **ful** or **less** to finish each word.

doubt_____   weight_____

mouth_____   color_____

pain_____   force_____

clue_____   cup_____

end_____   care_____

taste_____   rest_____

thank_____   beauti_____

grace_____   help_____

NOUN ★	VERB →	ADJECTIVE ☺	ADVERB ?
years	jumped	breathless	wildly
decades	jogged	fearful	softly
minutes	skipped	hopeless	sadly
seconds	danced	powerful	noisily

Showtime

Jack trembled as he waited backstage. In two _____ ★, he was going

onstage to sing. He had _____ → every day for _____ ★, so

he couldn't understand why he felt so _____ ☺. Jack took several deep

breaths. He thought about the song he was going to sing, but his mind suddenly froze!

"What am I going to do?" he thought. As his music began, Jack _____ →

_____ ? onstage. The auditorium was packed with people. Jack

began singing in a _____ ☺ and _____ ☺ voice. He

was grateful he remembered the words. When he finished his

song, everyone stood and cheered _____ ?,

"Bravo for the singer!" Jack grinned and bowed.

Suffixes

A **suffix** is a word part added to the end of a word.
It changes the meaning of the word.

ly = in a certain way
y = full of

| slow | slow**ly** | (in a slow way) |
| rain | rain**y** | (full of rain) |

Add **ly** or **y** to finish each word.

grouch_____   calm_____

eager_____   mood_____

smooth_____   sweat_____

bad_____   glad_____

brain_____   chill_____

leak_____   final_____

friend_____   bump_____

lone_____   cloud_____

NOUN ★	VERB →	ADJECTIVE ☺	ADVERB ?
potatoes	lose	gloomy	tenderly
pumpkins	swallow	funny	merrily
turkeys	throw	grumpy	eagerly
eggs	imagine	lucky	bitterly

The King's Road

Long ago, a king had a new road built. Before he opened the new road, he made a

_____ announcement. He decided he would _____ a
☺   →

contest to see who traveled the road best. The _____ winner would
                                                ☺

_____ ten gold _____ . On the contest day,
→   ★

everyone traveled the road. Some had beautiful chariots. Others walked. At the finish

line, many complained _____ about some _____
                       ?   ☺

rocks in the road, which slowed them down. Finally, a young girl crossed the

finish line and gave the king some shiny gold _____ .
                                               ★

"I removed some rocks from the road and found them

underneath," she explained _____ . "You're
                            ?

the winner!" announced the king.

VOCABULARY

Latin Roots

Some **roots**, such as **port**, **scrib**, **spect**, **struct**, **ven/vent**, and **vid/vis**, come from Latin.

That's a language that was spoken long ago.

You can use the root to figure out the meaning of the word.

Root	Meaning
<u>port</u>	carry
<u>scrib</u>	write
<u>spect</u>	see/look
<u>struct</u>	build
<u>ven</u>/<u>vent</u>	come
<u>vid</u>/<u>vis</u>	see

Put together the parts of each word and write them below.

ex + port = _____   de + struct + ion = _____

scrib + ble = _____   con + ven + tion = _____

spect + ator = _____   in + vis + ible = _____

Write a definition for three of the words above, using the **root** as a clue.

Word	Definition
_____	_____
_____	_____
_____	_____

NOUN	VERB	ADJECTIVE	ADVERB
★	➡	☺	?
nose	choked	weird	briefly
brain	collapsed	spectacular	slowly
ear	twirled	purple	regularly
mouth	boiled	important	quickly

Solar Eclipse

Have you ever seen a solar eclipse? If so, you probably _____ as
➡
you viewed this _____ event through _____
☺   ☺
glasses. A solar eclipse occurs when the sun's _____ is blocked.
★
Here's a description of what happens. The moon _____ moves
?
around Earth, but both Earth and the moon circle the sun. Sometimes the moon

_____ passes between the sun and Earth, but it's rare. When it
?
happens, the sun's light gets _____ by the moon. Both sky and Earth
➡
become dark. As the moon keeps moving, the _____
★
reappears. When is the next solar eclipse? Look it up

online, and then mark your calendar. You don't want to

miss this _____ show!
☺

Context Clues

Authors sometimes give clues to help a reader figure out the meaning of a new word. We call these **context clues**. There are many types of context clues. Here are a few:

Definition or Restatement: a definition of the word is given right after it, often in parentheses or followed by **is** or **means**

Synonym: a word with a similar meaning is given, often using the words **or**, **that is**, or **which is**

Example: lists of related things are given, and the word is often followed by **such as**, **include**, **these**, or **for example**

Word Part Clue: the reader can use prefixes, suffixes, and roots to figure out the meaning of the word

Read the sentence, focusing on the **boldfaced** word. Write the type of **context clue** given to help figure out its meaning.

1. _____ The **humongous**, or really big, dinosaur stomped through the forest.

2. _____ **Mammals**, such as bears, lions, and cows, give birth to live young.

Write a sentence for one of these words: **metamorphosis**, **tiny**, **independence**, **exhausted**. Provide a context clue to help your reader.

_____

_____

NOUN ★	VERB →	ADJECTIVE ☺	ADVERB ?
bunny	stolen	hurtful	terribly
spaceship	broken	evil	truly
cheetah	hidden	horrid	hugely
diamond	tickled	awful	somewhat

Mr. Slime's Crime

Lulu felt that Mr. Slime was guilty of carrying out the _____ ☺

crime. Based on his _____ ☺ character, she was guessing he had

_____ → the _____ ★ . Even though she was

_____ ? drowsy from her sleepless night, she searched for more

solid evidence, hard proof that Slime had done it. "I would bet Slime has also

_____ → the _____ ★ ," she thought.

"Only a thoughtless, uncaring person like him would act in this

_____ ? cruel, or unkind, way." Finally, Lulu

solved the mystery. Surprisingly, Slime had also snatched,

or quickly taken, the _____ ★ ! Everyone was

amazed and gave Lulu a _____ ★ .

Shades of Meaning: Verbs

Verbs are action words. Some verbs mean almost the same thing. However, each verb has a slightly different meaning.

nibbled	(ate by taking little bites)
ate	(ate normally)
devoured	(ate quickly)

Add a **verb** to finish each sentence: **whispered**, **said**, **screamed**.

1. "There's a giant spider on my arm!" she _____ .

2. He _____ the secret to me.

3. Mom _____ we had to wash the dishes after dinner.

Write a sentence with each word: **stroll**, **tiptoe**, **dash**.

1. _____

_____

_____

2. _____

_____

_____

3. _____

_____

_____

NOUN	VERB	ADJECTIVE	ADVERB
★	➡	😊	?
donkey	shuffled	strange	upstairs
clown	walked	angry	downstairs
noodle	sprinted	bored	nowhere
meatball	waddled	silly	somewhere

The Big Rat Race

The big Rat Race was starting. Devon buttoned up his rat costume and

_____ ➡ toward the gate. He felt _____ 😊 ,

but he would do anything to win the grand prize. Next to him, the other racers

looked _____ 😊 in their rat costumes. Bing! The starting bell rang,

and then they were off, madly racing _____ ? . Devon galloped as

fast as he could, picturing the _____ 😊 _____ ★ he

would win. Quickly, he _____ ➡ _____ ? . Panting

hard, he _____ ➡ toward the finish line before all the other racers.

"Yay!" cheered the crowd. "Three cheers for Devon

the _____ ★ !"

Shades of Meaning: Adjectives

Adjectives are describing words. Some adjectives mean almost the same thing. However, each adjective has a slightly different meaning.

large   (big)
giant   (very big)
enormous   (very, very big)

Add an **adjective** to finish each sentence: **cute**, **fuzzy**, **stunning**.

1. We watched the _____ sunset on the beach.

2. The baby was so _____ .

3. The _____ bird had feathers that looked like fire!

Write a sentence with each word: **afraid**, **spooked**, **terrified**.

1. _____

_____

_____

2. _____

_____

_____

3. _____

_____

_____

NOUN ★	VERB ➡	ADJECTIVE 😊	ADVERB ?
bananas	danced	brainy	boldly
cows	twirled	tricky	foolishly
diamonds	flipped	wise	noisily
airplanes	slept	sly	madly

Clever Chen

Once, _____ Chen sat in the shade of Ping's tree. "Leave!"
                    😊

Ping yelled _____ . "This is my tree!" "May I buy the
                    ?

shade?" Chen asked. "Sure," Ping said, grinning, and sold the shade for a bag of

_____ . As the sun moved across the sky, _____
        ★   😊

Chen _____ in Ping's yard. "Leave!" yelled Ping. "But
        ➡

I own the shade," _____ Chen replied. Then, Chen
                            😊

_____ in the shade on Ping's porch. "Leave!"
        ➡

screamed Ping _____ . "But I own the shade,"
                    ?

_____ Chen repeated. "You can buy it for
        😊

fifty bags of _____ ." Sadly, Ping
                ★

paid and was poor forever after.

Characters

The **characters** are whom the story is about. We learn about characters from what they say, think, and do. We also learn about them from how they feel and what motivates, or drives, them to do something.

Fill in the chart using information from your favorite stories.

Story:
Main Character:
What You Know About the Character and How:

Story:
Main Character:
What You Know About the Character and How:

NOUN	VERB	ADJECTIVE	ADVERB
★	→	☺	?
beetle	hollered	striped	Quietly
triangle	laughed	clever	Awkwardly
pickle	groaned	lemony	Hurriedly
hippopotamus	whispered	mushy	Instantly

The Tricky Treasure

Every day, Margo liked to hunt for treasure on her way to school. One day, she

picked up a tiny _____ (☺) _____ (★) . "You're late

again," Mrs. Olson _____ (→) when Margo finally arrived in class.

"You're the tardiest student in school." Margo glared at her textbook. "I wish I

wasn't a student," Margo _____ (→) as she rubbed her new treasure.

Poof! _____ (?) Margo turned into a _____ (☺)

_____ (★) ! All her classmates pointed at her and

_____ (→) . "This is worse than being a student,"

Margo _____ (→) . _____ (?) ,

Margo rubbed the treasure and turned back into herself.

"Whew!" she said.

Mood

Mood is the feeling a reader gets when reading a story. Authors use clear, exact, descriptive words to create the mood.

Read each set of sentences. How do you feel? Write the mood the author has set based on the words—sad, happy, scared, nervous, and so on.

1. It was a dark and stormy night. It was the kind of night when even

ghosts stay home. _____

_____

2. Carlos sat in the corner with his head down. Tears dripped from his

face. _____

_____

3. Mei quickly opened the box. Out popped a puppy with floppy ears

and a soft, wet nose. _____

_____

Write a sentence or two that shows a funny or silly mood.

_____

_____

Write a sentence or two that shows a scary or nervous mood.

_____

_____

NOUN ★	VERB →	ADJECTIVE ☺	ADVERB ?
trolls	sneered	strange	sloppily
witches	growled	frozen	grimly
skulls	cackled	creepy	hungrily
spiders	howled	wicked	angrily

The Bone-Chilling Bakery

Black clouds filled the sky. _____ wind whipped through the trees.
                                        ☺

A storm was coming, so Diego hurried inside the bakery. A _____
                                                                        ☺

baker oozed through some cobwebs to greet him. "What would you like?" she

_____ _____ . Diego's belly rumbled, but he
            →   ?

frowned at the _____ inside the glass display case. "Do you have any
                            ★

bread?" he asked _____ . "I have _____ ,
                            ?   ★

but no bread," the baker _____ . Diego shivered as a
                                    →

group of _____ _____ jumped out of the
                    ☺   ★

shadows. "Never mind," Diego stammered as he headed for the door. "I

think I'd rather starve!"

Moral of the Story

The **moral of a story** is the lesson of the story. It is something the writer wants the reader to learn. It is usually about how to be a better person, such as "always tell the truth" or "treat others as you want to be treated."

Fables are short stories that end with a moral. Read the name of each popular fable. Match the fable to the moral. You can look them up if you need to.

Fable	Moral
"The Crow and the Pitcher"	There is a time for work and a time for play.
"The Tortoise and the Hare"	Little friends can become great friends.
"The Ant and the Grasshopper"	Slow but steady wins the race, so never give up!
"The Lion and the Mouse"	Little by little does the trick; there is always a way.
"The North Wind and the Sun"	Kindness and persuasion, rather than force, always win people over.
"The Fox and the Crow"	Do not trust those who flatter you.

NOUN ★	VERB ➡	ADJECTIVE 😊	ADVERB ?
circus	snored	handsome	shyly
store	wept	soft	quietly
moon	groaned	super	gratefully
river	yelled	fancy	happily

The Wishful Woodpecker

Once, Woodpecker was jealous of Fox. "Fox is so _____ 😊," thought Woodpecker. "I want a _____ 😊 red coat like his." So, when Woodpecker saw Fox by the _____ ★ , he grabbed Fox's tail and petted it. "Your coat is so _____ 😊 !" Woodpecker _____ ➡ .

"But you must be so hot. If you take off your coat, I will gladly wear it for you."

"Thanks," _____ ➡ Fox. "Just let go of my tail, so I can pull my coat off for you." Woodpecker let go and waited _____ ? . But Fox just dashed off to the _____ ★ , and Woodpecker never saw him again.

Point of View

Point of view is how a story is told. It affects the information the reader gets from the story's narrator—the person telling the story.

First Person Point of View: The narrator, or person telling the story, is **in** the story. Key words used are **I** and **my**. We "hear" and "see" the story through the narrator's eyes only. Therefore, the information the narrator can provide is limited.

Third Person Point of View: The narrator, or person telling the story, is **not in** the story. We "hear" and "see" the story from an outside voice.

Fill in the chart using information from your favorite stories.

Story:	
Point of View:	**How You Know:**

Story:	
Point of View:	**How You Know:**

NOUN ★	VERB →	ADJECTIVE ☺	ADVERB ?
strawberries	painting	lazy	then
hammers	juggling	embarrassed	today
brooms	bouncing	snobby	once
oatmeal	attacking	polite	yesterday

Where's the Wolf?

I was tired of tending sheep. But _____ **?** , I played a trick.

"Wolf!" I cried. "There's a wolf _____ **→** the sheep!" It

was so funny to see the _____ ☺ villagers come running with

their _____ **★** . "Whoops," I told them. "Unfortunately, the

_____ ☺ wolf just ran off!"

The shepherd yawned in the meadow. _____ **?** , he decided

to make things interesting. "A wolf is _____ **→** the sheep!"

he yelled. He laughed when he saw the _____ ☺ villagers

charging up the hill holding _____ **★** . "Sorry," he said.

"You just missed him. But the _____ ☺ guy ran that way!"

Main Ideas

The **main ideas** are the most important facts in a text.

Book Title: *Dinosaurs*

Main Ideas:

1. They lived millions of years ago.
2. Scientists have found their bones and fossils.
3. They are all now extinct.

Read the main ideas. Write a title for this book.

Book Title: _____

Main Ideas:

1. It orbits, or travels around, Earth.

2. It can be seen in the night sky, but changes shape
   at different times of the month.

3. Astronauts first traveled to it in 1969.

Write a title for a book. Include three details that might be found in
the book.

Book Title: _____

Main Ideas:

1. _____

2. _____

3. _____

NOUN ★	VERB →	ADJECTIVE 😊	ADVERB ?
fish	dance	awesome	Usually
pizza	cook	amazing	Often
kittens	sing	wild	Sometimes
chicks	clean	lovable	Normally

Fabulous Feet

What bird nests on land, searches for food in the sea, and has _____
😊

blue feet? The blue-footed booby! _____ , these birds live along the
?

coast in Central and South America. The _____ color of their feet
😊

comes from their diet of fresh _____ . _____ ,
★ ?

males tend to have brighter feet than females, and the healthiest, well-fed males

have the brightest blue feet of all. The males do a clumsy dance with their feet to attract

_____ . The females like it when the males _____ !
★ →

These birds also use their

webbed feet to cover their

_____ and
★

keep them warm.

 **ANSWER KEY**

---

6 · PHONICS AND WORD STUDY

Long Vowels

Each **long vowel** sound says the vowel's name.
Each sound can be spelled many ways.

long a	train, play, sleigh, great, table, space
long e	street, leaf, field, we, key, happy
long i	bright, tie, cry, kite, child
long o	goat, snow, rope, go, toes
long u	few, music, mule, argue

Add a **long vowel** spelling to finish each picture name.

birthd **a y**   p **a i** ntbrush

sixt **e e** n **16**   p **e a** nut

kn **i g h** t   cr **y** ing

pill **o w**   sailb **o a** t

m **u** seum   c **u b e**

---

8 · PHONICS AND WORD STUDY

r-Controlled Vowels

When the letter **r** follows a vowel, it changes the vowel's sound.
The spellings **er, ir,** and **ur** stand for the same sounds.

fern   shirt   burning

These words have **r-controlled** vowel sounds and spellings, too.

corn   more   roar   star   hair   share   pear

Add an **r-controlled** vowel spelling to finish each picture name.

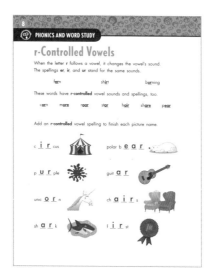

c **i r** cus   polar b **e a r**

p **u r** ple   guit **a r**

unic **o r** n   ch **a i r** s

sh **a r** k   f **i r** st

---

10 · PHONICS AND WORD STUDY

Diphthongs

Some vowel sounds feel like they move around in your mouth.
These spellings stand for those sounds.

b**oy**   sp**oi**led   s**ou**th   fr**ow**ning

Add one of the above spellings to finish each picture name.

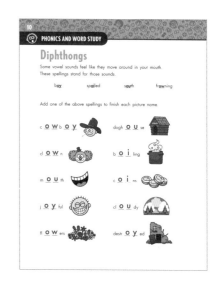

c **o w** b **o y**   dogh **o u** se

cl **o w** n   b **o i** ling

m **o u** th   c **o i** ns

j **o y** ful   cl **o u** dy

fl **o w** ers   destr **o y** ed

---

12 · PHONICS AND WORD STUDY

Variant Vowels

The vowel sound in **moon** can be spelled many ways.

sp**oo**n   gl**ue**   gr**ou**p   ch**ew**   J**u**ne

The vowel sound in **good** can be spelled many ways.

st**oo**d   sh**ou**ld   p**u**sh

The vowel sound in **all** can be spelled many ways.

str**aw**   l**au**nching   s**al**t   sm**all**est   t**al**king   b**ou**ght   t**au**ght

Add one of the above spellings to finish each picture name.

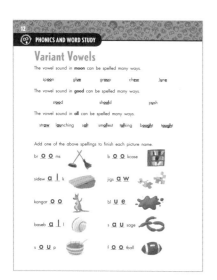

br **o o** ms   b **o o** kcase

sidew **a l** k   jigs **a w**

kangar **o o**   bl **u e**

baseb **a l** l   s **a u** sage

s **o u** p   f **o o** tball

---

14 · PHONICS AND WORD STUDY

Closed Syllables

A **closed syllable** ends in a consonant and has a short vowel sound.
Knowing this can help you chunk and read longer words.

lit/tle   nap/kin

Add the missing **closed syllable**.

k **i t** ten   fos **s i l**

r **a b** bit   chick **e n**

b l **a n k** et   in s **e c t**

p **u m p** kin   pen **c i l**

s **u b** tract 10 – 2 = 8   den **t i s t**

---

16 · PHONICS AND WORD STUDY

Open Syllables

An **open syllable** ends in a vowel and has a long vowel sound.
Knowing this can help you chunk and read longer words.

se/cret   fi/nal

Add the missing **open syllable**.

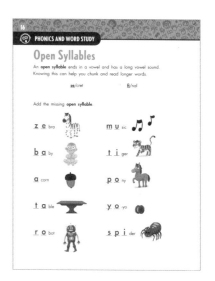

z **e** bra   m **u** sic

b **a** by   t **i** ger

a corn   p **o** ny

t **a** ble   y **o** -yo

r **o** bot   s p **i** der

---

18 · PHONICS AND WORD STUDY

Final Stable Syllables

Some **syllables** are common at the ends of words.
Looking for these syllables can help you chunk and read longer words.

Consonant + le	Other
bat/tle	lo/tion
fa/ble	mis/sion
han/dle	cap/ture
gig/gle	pres/sure

Add the missing **final syllable**.

poo **d l e**   televi **s i o n**

ea **g l e**   erup **t i o n**

bot **t l e**   pic **t u r e**

puz **z l e**   trea **s u r e**

---

20 · PHONICS AND WORD STUDY

Using Prefixes to Sound Out Words

A **prefix** is a word part added to the beginning of a word,
such as **un** and **re**.
Quickly seeing these common word parts can help you chunk
and read longer words.

unhappy   **re**write   **dis**agree   **mis**use

Circle the **prefix** in each word.

un)do   re)read   dis)like

pre)cook   mis)read   mid)afternoon

re)wrapped   dis)obey   un)packing

---

22 · PHONICS AND WORD STUDY

Using Suffixes to Sound Out Words

A **suffix** is a word part added to the end of a word,
such as **ed** and **ful**.
Quickly seeing these common word parts can help you
chunk and read longer words.

plant**ed**   use**ful**   hope**less**

Circle the **suffix** or **suffixes** in each word.

send(ed   use(less   strand(ed

order(ed   sudden(ly   care(less(ness

dark(ness   beauti(ful(ly   help(ful

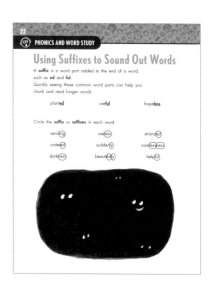

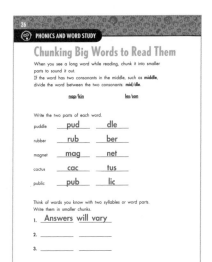

24 PHONICS AND WORD STUDY

Reading Words with Latin Suffixes

A **suffix** is a word part added to the end of a word.
Some suffixes, such as **able**, **ible**, **ation**, **ment**, **ty**, and **ity**, come from Latin.
That's a language that was spoken long ago.

Noun	Adjective
cre**ation**	siz**able**
state**ment**	flex**ible**
certain**ty**	
similar**ity**	

Add the **suffix** to each word to make a new word. Sometimes the spelling changes. Sometimes the pronunciation changes, too.

inform + ation = **information**
loyal + ty = **loyalty**
govern + ment = **government**
like + able = **likable**
amaze + ment = **amazement**
electric + ity = **electricity**
comfort + able = **comfortable**
reverse + ible = **reversible**

26 PHONICS AND WORD STUDY

Chunking Big Words to Read Them

When you see a long word while reading, chunk it into smaller parts to sound it out.
If the word has two consonants in the middle, such as **middle**, divide the word between the two consonants: **mid/dle**.

nap/kin   les/son

Write the two parts of each word.

puddle   **pud**   **dle**
rubber   **rub**   **ber**
magnet   **mag**   **net**
cactus   **cac**   **tus**
public   **pub**   **lic**

Think of words you know with two syllables or word parts.
Write them in smaller chunks.

1. **Answers will vary**
2. _____ _____
3. _____ _____

28 PHONICS AND WORD STUDY

Reading Big Words Strategy

When you see a long word while reading, use these five steps to chunk it into smaller parts to read it.

Step 1: Look for common word parts at the beginning, such as prefixes (**un**, **re**, **dis**, **mis**).
Step 2: Look for common word parts at the end, such as suffixes (**ing**, **ed**, **ful**, **less**).
Step 3: Look at what's left. Use what you know about sounding out words and syllable types to chunk it.
Step 4: Sound out all the word parts slowly. It will be close to the real word.
Step 5: Say the word parts fast. Adjust your pronunciation to say it correctly.

Check the steps you use to figure out these words. Write the meaning of each word.

rereading
☑ Step 1
☑ Step 2
☑ Step 3
☑ Step 4
☑ Step 5
Meaning:
reading again

unhelpful
☑ Step 1
☑ Step 2
☑ Step 3
☑ Step 4
☑ Step 5
Meaning:
not full of help

30 PHONICS AND WORD STUDY

Read Irregularly Spelled Words

Most words in English can be sounded out using what you know about common letters, spellings, and sounds. However, there are some words that don't follow the rules. These words need special attention. Follow these steps to learn these words.

Step 1: Read the word. Say the sounds you hear in it.
Step 2: Spell the word out loud.
Step 3: Write the word as you say the letter names.

Use the three steps to practice the words below. Check the box after completing Steps 1 and 2. Write the word for Step 3.

was	Step 1 ☑	Step 2 ☑	Step 3 **was**
one	Step 1 ☑	Step 2 ☑	Step 3 **one**
there	Step 1 ☑	Step 2 ☑	Step 3 **there**
where	Step 1 ☑	Step 2 ☑	Step 3 **where**
come	Step 1 ☑	Step 2 ☑	Step 3 **come**
some	Step 1 ☑	Step 2 ☑	Step 3 **some**
would	Step 1 ☑	Step 2 ☑	Step 3 **would**
should	Step 1 ☑	Step 2 ☑	Step 3 **should**
give	Step 1 ☑	Step 2 ☑	Step 3 **give**
have	Step 1 ☑	Step 2 ☑	Step 3 **have**

32 WRITING: Spelling, Grammar, and Story Structure

Inflectional Endings with Spelling Changes

When you add **s**, **es**, **ed**, or **ing** to a word, you sometimes have to change the spelling before adding the ending.

1. Double the final consonant
stop   stops   sto**pp**ed   sto**pp**ing

2. Drop e
save   saves   sav**ed**   sav**ing**

3. Change y to i
cry   cr**ies**   cr**ied**   crying

Add **s**, **ed**, and **ing** to each word.

	Add **s** or **es**	Add **ed**	Add **ing**
tap	**taps**	**tapped**	**tapping**
bake	**bakes**	**baked**	**baking**
reply	**replies**	**replied**	**replying**

34 WRITING: Spelling, Grammar, and Story Structure

Spelling Multisyllabic Words

When spelling a longer word, it is easier to chunk it into smaller parts or syllables. Then spell each part, one at a time. Think about other words you know with these same or similar parts.

Break each word into syllables. Write each syllable in the blanks.

railroad   **rail** **road**
misreading   **mis** **read** **ing**
independence   **in** **de** **pen** **dence**
unexpected   **un** **ex** **pect** **ed**

Look at each picture. Say the picture name. Write each word part by part (syllable by syllable).

 mag **net**

 vol **ca** **no**

 di **no** **saur**

 cat **er** **pil** **lar**

36 WRITING: Spelling, Grammar, and Story Structure

Irregular Plural Nouns

A **plural** word is more than one of something.
Most naming words, or nouns, add **s** or **es** to make it plural.
However, some plural words do not. We call these irregular.

Regular

1 train 2 trains   1 box 2 box**es**

Irregular

1 woman 2 women   1 mouse 2 mice

Write the **plural** of each word.

1 foot	2 **feet**	1 man	2 **men**
1 goose	2 **geese**	1 person	2 **people**
1 knife	2 **knives**	1 child	2 **children**
1 tooth	2 **teeth**	1 sheep	2 **sheep**

38 WRITING: Spelling, Grammar, and Story Structure

Pronoun-Antecedent Agreement

A **pronoun** is a word that takes the place of a noun. Words like **he**, **she**, **it**, and **they** are pronouns.
Writers use pronouns to avoid saying the noun over and over. It makes their writing more interesting.

An **antecedent** is the word the pronoun refers to. For example, read the sentences below. The pronoun is **it** and **dog** is the antecedent. The word **it** takes the place of the noun **dog**.

The <u>dog</u> is fluffy. <u>It</u> is also black.

A **singular** (meaning "one") **pronoun** takes the place of a singular noun. Singular pronouns include **he**, **she**, **you**, and **it**.

A **plural** (meaning "more than one") **pronoun** takes the place of a plural noun. Plural pronouns include **we** and **they**.

Add the correct **pronoun**.

1. The man wears a black suit with a purple tie. **He** is very tall.
2. My sister and I bought a microwave for our mother. **We** got it on sale.
3. Mrs. Chen is a great storyteller. **She** told us a traditional tale from China.
4. The dog leaped into air. **It/He/She** looked like a superhero.
5. The children played soccer at recess. **They** had tons of fun!

ANSWER KEY

Adjectives

An **adjective** is a describing word. It tells more about something.

a bear a **little black** bear a **big angry** bear

Add **adjectives** to finish each sentence. **Answers will vary**

1. The _____ stars lit up the night sky like diamonds.
2. My dog Scruffles is _____ and _____.
3. The _____ giraffe nibbled on the _____ leaves at the top of the tree.
4. When I see a _____ insect, I run the other way!
5. A _____ movie is my favorite, but I don't enjoy _____ ones.
6. The _____ children raced through the hallways.
7. My coat was _____, but now it's old and _____.

Adverbs

An **adverb** is a word that tells more about a verb. It can tell how, when, or where.

We shouted **loudly**. (how)
We went to a restaurant **yesterday**. (when)
We played soccer **outside**. (where)

Adverbs that compare two things end in **er** or add **more**.
José worked **harder** than his big brother.
Marko ran **more slowly** than his best friend.

Adverbs that compare three or more things end in **est** or add **most**.
Martina ran the **fastest** of all her classmates.
That was the **most quietly** we ever watched TV.

Add one of these **adverbs** to finish each sentence:
slower, fastest, more loudly, most joyfully

1. Tomás shouted **more loudly** than his sister Graciela.
2. Is a turtle **slower** than a frog?
3. A cheetah is the **fastest** animal I have ever seen!
4. We sang the **most joyfully** of all the holiday choirs.

Abstract Nouns

Most nouns are things you can see, like **baby**, **butterfly**, or **balloon**. However, some nouns you can't see, hear, taste, touch, or smell. We call these **abstract nouns**. They stand for concepts like **freedom** and **curiosity**.

Complete each sentence with one of these abstract nouns:
ability, appetite, bravery, friendship, goal, kindness, success.

1. She has the **ability** to sing and tumble at the same time!
2. My **friendship** with my sister is very important to me.
3. The firefighters' **bravery** helped to save the family from the blaze.
4. He showed great **kindness** when he helped the elderly lady cross the street.
5. Our **success** in winning the competition depends on hard work and skill.
6. My **goal** is to become a doctor someday.
7. Whenever I smell pizza, my **appetite** seems to grow bigger!

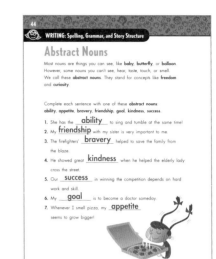

Conjunctions

A **conjunction** is a word that connects (or joins) words, parts of sentences, and sentences. Think of them as glue words. You can remember the seven main conjunctions by remembering this:

FANBOYS

For The goat must have been very hungry, **for** he gobbled her food.
And We play soccer **and** volleyball at school.
Nor Neither my mom **nor** my dad drink tomato juice.
But After the race, I felt tired **but** happy.
Or Do you want pepperoni **or** olives on your pizza?
Yet It was early, **yet** we all wanted to eat dinner.
So I am tired, **so** I think I'll skip that TV show tonight.

Add a **conjunction** to complete each sentence.

1. We will eat hamburgers **and** hot dogs at our cookout.
2. Do you prefer summer **or** winter?
3. My dog ate a big bowl of food, **but/yet** still seemed hungry.
4. Neither my sister **nor** I have green eyes like our mother.
5. I have tons of homework, **so** I will have to focus to finish it.

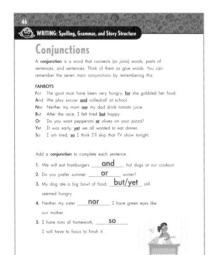

Irregular Past Tense Verbs

Most **past tense verbs** end in **ed**.
Today, I **walk** to the store. (present)
Last week, I **walked** to the store. (past)

However, some verbs do not. We call these irregular.
Today, I **drink** orange juice. (present)
Yesterday, I **drank** a glass of milk. (past)

Finish each sentence with the **past tense** form of each verb.

1. (buy) Yesterday, I **bought** a new notebook for school.
2. (build) Last year, they **built** a new mall in our town.
3. (leave) Yesterday, she **left** that package for you.
4. (catch) Last week, I **caught** a very bad cold.
5. (spend) Yesterday, I **spent** twenty dollars on a new shirt.
6. (hear) One time, I **heard** a strange noise in the attic.

Subject-Verb Agreement

The **subject** and **verb** of a sentence must both be singular (showing one) or both be plural (showing more than one). They must "agree."

The **elephant stomps** through the mud.
(elephant = one elephant = singular)
(stomps, as in "it stomps" = singular)

The **elephants stomp** through the mud.
(elephants = more than one elephant = plural)
(stomp, as in "they stomp" = plural)

Write the **verb** that best fits each sentence. Make sure the subject and the verb "agree."

1. The dog **gobbles** his food. (gobble/gobbles)
2. We **race** around the playground. (race/races)
3. The children **gather** to watch the movie. (gather/gathers)
4. Mom and Dad **shop** at the market on Saturdays. (shop/shops)
5. When a volcano **explodes**, it spews lava. (explode/explodes)
6. Those cars **run** on electricity. (run/runs)
7. Pencils **are** my favorite writing tool. (is/are)

Compound Sentences

A **compound sentence** has two sentences put together. The words **and**, **but**, **or**, and **so** are used to make a compound sentence. A comma (**,**) is put before one of these words.

Mark played soccer, **and** I read a book.
I like to sleep late, **but** I have to get up early tomorrow.

Put together the two sentences to make a **compound sentence**.

I play soccer. My brother plays basketball.
I play soccer, and my brother plays basketball.

We like to eat candy. Our school doesn't allow it.
We like to eat candy, but our school doesn't allow it.

Complex Sentences

A **complex sentence** has an **independent clause** (a complete sentence) and a **dependent clause** (not a complete sentence and cannot stand on its own). The **dependent clause** begins with a word like **after**, **although**, **as**, **because**, **before**, **even though**, **unless**, **whenever**, and **wherever**.

Our democracy works because people have the right to vote.
independent clause | dependent clause

Add a **dependent clause** to make a **complex sentence**.

I want to go home. **Answers will vary. Sample answer might include: I want to go home because I am tired.**

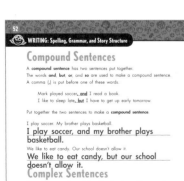

Possessives

A **possessive noun** shows who or what owns something. Add **'s** to a noun that names one thing (singular noun).

This is the grizzly **bear's** cave.

Add just an **'** to a noun that names more than one thing, and ends in **s** (plural noun).

The three **boys'** rooms are filled with books.

If a plural noun does NOT end in **s**, add **'s**.

The **men's** team rode the bus to the game.

Fix each sentence.

1. The scientists found a dinosaur **'s** bones.
2. All four dogs **'** food was kept under the sink.
3. The women **'s** hats were on sale.
4. The children **'s** games are kept in the closet.
5. My mom **'s** favorite cake is chocolate with strawberries.
6. The school **'s** principal greets the students each morning.

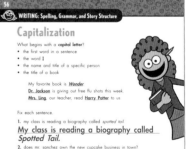

Capitalization

What begins with a **capital letter**?
• the first word in a sentence
• the word **I**
• the name and title of a specific person
• the title of a book

My favorite book is **Wonder**.
Dr. Jackson is giving out free flu shots this week.
Mrs. Ling, our teacher, read **Harry Potter** to us.

Fix each sentence.

1. my class is reading a biography called *spotted tail*.
My class is reading a biography called Spotted Tail.
2. does mr. sanchez own the new cupcake business in town?
Does Mr. Sanchez own the new cupcake business in town?
3. *stuart little* is a book about a mouse.
Stuart Little is a book about a mouse.
4. i just finished reading *charlotte's web* and cried.
I just finished reading Charlotte's Web and cried.
5. i hope gov. mitchum will visit our school.
I hope Gov. Mitchum will visit our school.

Panel 58

WRITING: Spelling, Grammar, and Story Structure

Commas in Quotations

Use a **comma** to separate a direct quote and who is saying it. The comma appears **before** the quotation mark (").

"I am running late for school," said Daniel.
My mother yelled, "Hurry up!"

Add the missing **comma** in each sentence.

1. "Please help me," said the boy.
2. "I really want to play soccer today," said Juan Carlos.
3. The mouse ran from the owl, screeching, "Eek!"
4. Li said, "My favorite movies are action films."

Commas in Addresses

Use a **comma** in an address to separate the city from the state.

Lupé Lopez
12 East 34th Street
Springfield, AZ 56789

Write a school's address below.

_____ Answers will vary
_____
_____

Panel 60

WRITING: Spelling, Grammar, and Story Structure

Quotes

Use **quotation marks** when quoting the exact words someone says.

"I will be late to the party," said Dr. Velazquez.
The giant screamed, "Fee, fi, fo, fum!"

Add the missing **quotation marks** in each sentence.

1. "I hope we order pizza after the game," said the boy.
2. "We can shop at the mall tomorrow," said Mom.
3. "What are you reading this week?" asked Mrs. Jung.
4. "Help! Help!" shouted the man. "My house is on fire!"

Write sentences showing a conversation between you and a friend or family member.

1. _____ Answers will vary
2. _____
3. _____
4. _____

Panel 62

WRITING: Spelling, Grammar, and Story Structure

Text Structure: Sequence

Writers of informational text use different ways to **structure** their writing. One way is to put the information in **sequence**, or **time order**.

These signal words often alert a reader that the text is organized this way: **first, second, third, next, then, last, after, finally, before, in the beginning, to start, meanwhile, in the middle, at the end**. The writer might also use **dates in order** (such as 1776, 1865, and 2020).

Fill in the **sequence** paragraph. Write about an interesting topic, like cooking something or making a craft.

The **first** step in making _____ Answers will vary
_____ is to _____

After that, you must _____
_____

Next, you need to _____
_____

Finally, you _____
_____

Panel 64

WRITING: Spelling, Grammar, and Story Structure

Text Structure: Cause/Effect

Writers of informational text use different ways to **structure** their writing. One way is to explain the **causes** and **effects** of something. The causes are **why** something happens. The effects are **what** happens.

These signal words often alert a reader that the text is organized this way: **because, cause, effect, therefore, if…then, as a result, due to, reason, since, leads to, as a consequence, consequently.**

Fill in the **cause and effect** paragraph. Write about an interesting topic, like climate change or invasive animals attacking plants and animals in an environment.

Because of _____ , _____ Answers will vary
_____
_____ has happened.

Therefore, _____
_____
_____

This explains why _____
_____
_____

Panel 66

VOCABULARY

Prefixes

A **prefix** is a word part added to the beginning of a word. It changes the meaning of the word.

un, in = not, the opposite of
re = again

happy	**un**happy	(not happy)
visible	**in**visible	(not visible)
read	**re**read	(read again)

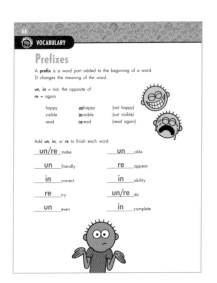

Add **un**, **in**, or **re** to finish each word.

un/re make	un able
un friendly	re appear
in correct	in ability
re try	un/re do
un even	in complete

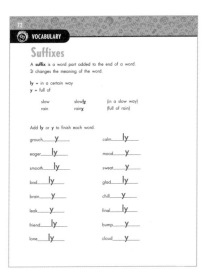

Panel 68

VOCABULARY

Prefixes

A **prefix** is a word part added to the beginning of a word. It changes the meaning of the word.

dis, il = not, the opposite of
mis = bad, wrong, incorrectly

like	**dis**like	(the opposite of like)
treat	**mis**treat	(treat badly or wrongly)
logical	**il**logical	(not logical)

Add **dis**, **mis**, or **il** to finish each word.

dis agree	il legal
dis obey	dis able
mis understood	dis appear
dis order	il legible
mis lead	dis/mis place
mis heard	dis/mis trust
mis judge	il literate
dis honest	mis print

Panel 70

VOCABULARY

Suffixes

A **suffix** is a word part added to the end of a word. It changes the meaning of the word.

ful = full of, with
less = without, not

| fear | fear**ful** | (full of fear) |
| hope | hope**less** | (without hope) |

Add **ful** or **less** to finish each word.

doubt less/ful	weight less
mouth ful	color less/ful
pain less/ful	force ful
clue less	cup ful
end less	care less/ful
taste less/ful	rest less/ful
thank less/ful	beauti ful
grace less/ful	help less/ful

Panel 72

VOCABULARY

Suffixes

A **suffix** is a word part added to the end of a word. It changes the meaning of the word.

ly = in a certain way
y = full of

| slow | slow**ly** | (in a slow way) |
| rain | rain**y** | (full of rain) |

Add **ly** or **y** to finish each word.

grouch y	calm ly
eager ly	mood y
smooth ly	sweat y
bad ly	glad ly
brain y	chill y
leak y	final ly
friend ly	bump y
lone ly	cloud y

Panel 74

VOCABULARY

Latin Roots

Some roots, such as **port, scrib, spect, struct, ven/vent,** and **vid/vis**, come from Latin.
That's a language that was spoken long ago.
You can use the root to figure out the meaning of the word.

Root	Meaning
port	carry
scrib	write
spect	see/look
struct	build
ven/vent	come
vid/vis	see

Put together the parts of each word and write them below.

ex + port = **export**   de + struct + ion = **destruction**

scrib + ble = **scribble**   con + ven + tion = **convention**

spect + ator = **spectator**   in + vis + ible = **invisible**

Write a definition for three of the words above, using the **root** as a clue.

Word	Definition
Answers will vary	

ANSWER KEY

---

76 VOCABULARY

Context Clues

Authors sometimes give clues to help a reader figure out the meaning of a new word. We call these **context clues**. There are many types of context clues. Here are a few:

Definition or Restatement: a definition of the word is given right after it, often in parentheses or followed by **is** or **means**

Synonym: a word with a similar meaning is given, often using the words **or, that is,** or **which is**

Example: lists of related things are given, and the word is often followed by **such as, include, these,** or **for example**

Word Part Clue: the reader can use prefixes, suffixes, and roots to figure out the meaning of the word

Read the sentence, focusing on the **boldfaced** word. Write the type of **context clue** given to help figure out its meaning.

1. **synonym** The **humongous,** or really big, dinosaur stomped through the forest.

2. **example** **Mammals,** such as bears, lions, and cows, give birth to live young.

Write a sentence for one of these words: **metamorphosis, tiny, independence, exhausted.** Provide a context clue to help your reader.

Answers will vary

---

78 VOCABULARY

Shades of Meaning: Verbs

Verbs are action words. Some verbs mean almost the same thing. However, each verb has a slightly different meaning.

nibbled	(ate by taking little bites)
ate	(ate normally)
devoured	(ate quickly)

Add a **verb** to finish each sentence: **whispered, said, screamed.**

1. "There's a giant spider on my arm!" she **screamed**

2. He **whispered** the secret to me.

3. Mom **said** we had to wash the dishes after dinner.

Write a sentence with each word: **stroll, tiptoe, dash.**

1. **Answers will vary**

2. _____

3. _____

---

80 VOCABULARY

Shades of Meaning: Adjectives

Adjectives are describing words. Some adjectives mean almost the same thing. However, each adjective has a slightly different meaning.

large	(big)
giant	(very big)
enormous	(very, very big)

Add an adjective to finish each sentence: **cute, fuzzy, stunning.**

1. We watched the **stunning** sunset on the beach.

2. The baby was so **cute**

3. The **fuzzy** bird had feathers that looked like fire!

Write a sentence with each word: **afraid, spooked, terrified.**

1. **Answers will vary**

2. _____

3. _____

---

82 VOCABULARY

Characters

The **characters** are whom the story is about. We learn about characters from what they say, think, and do. We also learn about them from how they feel and what motivates, or drives, them to do something.

Fill in the chart using information from your favorite stories.

Story:	Answers will vary
Main Character:	
What You Know About the Character and How:	

Story:	Answers will vary
Main Character:	
What You Know About the Character and How:	

---

84 VOCABULARY

Mood

Mood is the feeling a reader gets when reading a story. Authors use clear, exact, descriptive words to create the mood.

Read each set of sentences. How do you feel? Write the mood the author has set based on the words—sad, happy, scared, nervous, and so on.

1. It was a dark and stormy night. It was the kind of night when even ghosts stay home. **Answers will vary, but might include: scared**

2. Carlos sat in the corner with his head down. Tears dripped from his face. **Answers will vary, but might include: sad**

3. Mei quickly opened the box. Out popped a puppy with floppy ears and a soft, wet nose. **Answers will vary, but might include: happy**

Write a sentence or two that shows a funny or silly mood.

Answers will vary

Write a sentence or two that shows a scary or nervous mood.

Answers will vary

---

86 VOCABULARY

Moral of the Story

The **moral of a story** is the lesson of the story. It is something the writer wants the reader to learn. It is usually about how to be a better person, such as "always tell the truth" or "treat others as you want to be treated."

Fables are short stories that end with a moral. Read the name of each popular fable. Match the fable to the moral. You can look them up if you need to.

Fable	Moral
"The Crow and the Pitcher"	There is a time for work and a time for play.
"The Tortoise and the Hare"	Little friends can become great friends.
"The Ant and the Grasshopper"	Slow but steady wins the race, so never give up!
"The Lion and the Mouse"	Little by little does the trick; there is always a way.
"The North Wind and the Sun"	Kindness and persuasion, rather than force, always win people over.
"The Fox and the Crow"	Do not trust those who flatter you.

---

88 VOCABULARY

Point of View

Point of view is how a story is told. It affects the information the reader gets from the story's narrator—the person telling the story.

First Person Point of View: The narrator, or person telling the story, is **in** the story. Key words used are **I** and **my.** We "hear" and "see" the story through the narrator's eyes only. Therefore, the information the narrator can provide is limited.

Third Person Point of View: The narrator, or person telling the story, is **not** in the story. We "hear" and "see" the story from an outside voice.

Fill in the chart using information from your favorite stories.

Story: Answers will vary	
Point of View:	How You Know:

Story: Answers will vary	
Point of View:	How You Know:

---

90 VOCABULARY

Main Ideas

The **main ideas** are the most important facts in a text.

Book Title: _Dinosaurs_

Main Ideas:

1. They lived millions of years ago.
2. Scientists have found their bones and fossils.
3. They are all now extinct.

Read the main ideas. Write a title for this book.

Book Title: Answers will vary,

Main Ideas: but might include: The Moon

1. It orbits, or travels around, Earth.
2. It can be seen in the night sky, but changes shape at different times of the month.
3. Astronauts first traveled to it in 1969.

Write a title for a book. Include three details that might be found in the book.

Book Title: Answers will vary

Main Ideas:

1. _____
2. _____
3. _____